Giddy the Great

For Isabel,

who is scared of nothing

J.R.

For my brother, Philip

L.C.

ORCHARD BOOKS
338 Euston Road, London NW1 3BH
Orchard Books Australia
17/207 Kent Street, Sydney NSW 2000

ISBN 978 1 84616 489 7

First published in 2006 by Orchard Books
First published in paperback in 2007

Text © Jamie Rix 2006
Illustrations © Lynne Chapman 2006

The right of Jamie Rix to be identified as the author and Lynne Chapman to be identified as the illustrator
of this work has been asserted by them in accordance with the Copyright, Designs and Patents Act, 1988.

A CIP catalogue record for this book is available from the British Library.

2 4 6 8 10 9 7 5 3 1

Printed in Singapore

Orchard Books is a division of Hachette Children's Books

Giddy the Great

Jamie Rix

Lynne Chapman

ORCHARD BOOKS

Giddy Goat climbed everything.

Small hills,

leaning trees,

stone walls . . .

. . . and even a craggy old ram called Ramilles.

And everywhere that Giddy climbed –
his best friend, Edmund, climbed too.

But Edmund was
a woolly mutton
and there were
some places his
meadow-made
hooves would
not stick.

As Giddy climbed
higher and higher,
Edmund had to
watch from below.

"If you keep leaving Edmund behind you'll lose him as a friend," warned Giddy's mother. "And best friends don't grow on trees."

"But I'm training for The Giant Pinnacle Race!" said Giddy. "First goat to the top is the winner!"

The
Giant
Pinnacle
was a
s
o
a
r
i
n
g
broom
handle
of a rock
that was
said to
hold up
the sky.

"I can't climb that!" quaked Edmund.

"Don't be such a **scaredy-cat!**" shouted Giddy. "Let's practise for the race so that I can win and everyone will call me Giddy the Great!"

Edmund didn't want to let his friend down, but the rock was too steep for him. He slipped back down into the low-lying meadows . . .

. . . . while Giddy Goat set off around the world to practise climbing really high things.

Giddy went to
the big city and
climbed bridges
and skyscrapers.

He went to Paris
and climbed the
Eiffel Tower.

And to London to climb
Nelson's Column . . .

... and to New York City where he climbed the Empire State Building right to the very top.

Move over King Kong, here comes Giddy the Great!

But even though
Giddy was standing
on top of the world,
he was lonely.

He missed
his best friend,
Edmund, and wanted
to say sorry for
calling him a
scaredy-cat.

So Giddy sent a note by Postal Pigeon –

COMING HOME TODAY!

– and headed for home, just in time . . .

Edmund was waiting for him with exciting news. "I'm going to take part in The Giant Pinnacle Race!" he said.

"Edmund," Giddy gulped,
"there's something I've got
to say to you. I'm s . . .
I'm s . . ."
It was hard
saying sorry . . .

The Giant Pinnacle Race
START

. . . but just then, Pa Billy called
all the goats (and one mutton)
to the starting line.

"I'd like to welcome Edmund,"
the old goat said, "as the
first mutton ever to climb
The Giant Pinnacle! Brave boy!

First one to the top wins!"
he shouted.

Giant Pinnacle
START

"GO!"

There was a
mad rush!

Giddy was first to arrive,

skittering

up the mountain's
craggy face like a fly.
The other goats were close
behind, but Edmund
trailed in last.

"Are you all right?" shouted Giddy.

"Don't worry about me!" said Edmund.

But he was stuck.

Giddy knew what he had to do!

With only inches to go before the finishing line, Giddy turned and leapt back down the mountain.

"What are you doing?" shouted Edmund. "You were **winning!**"

"But I have won," said Giddy.

Edmund looked puzzled. "How do you mean?"

"I may have lost the race," said Giddy, "but I've found my best friend again!"

Later that night, while the moon played peekaboo with the mountain, the goats and the muttons

threw a party to celebrate the race.
Ramilles the Ram-Jam and 'Puffing' Pa Billy
rocked the stars with their Alpine Horns

while Giddy
and Edmund
sat by the fire
and talked.

"Thank you for saving me," said Edmund.
"You are Giddy the Great after all!"
"Not always," said Giddy. "Sometimes
I can be rather selfish."
He took a deep breath.

"I was wrong to call you a scaredy-cat,"
he said. "So I want to say . . .

. . . that I'm trying to
say, Edward . . .

. . . what I'm trying
to say is that . . .

"No!" giggled Giddy.
"I'm **sorry!**"

And once he had said it,
Giddy Goat really did feel great!